Acknowledgements

....

Thanks are due to the School of Literature, Drama and Creative Writing at UEA in partnership with Egg Box Publishing for making this anthology possible.

We'd also like to thank the following people:

Moniza Alvi, Amit Chaudhuri, Andrew Cowan, William Fiennes, Giles Foden, Sarah Gooderson, Lavinia Greenlaw, Rachel Hore, Kathryn Hughes, Katie Konyn, Daniel Leeson, Michael Lengsfield, Jean McNeil, Natalie Mitchell, Beatrice Poubeau, Rob Ritchie, Michèle Roberts, James Scudamore, Ali Smith, Helen Smith, Henry Sutton, George Szirtes, Val Taylor, Steve Waters and Peter Womack.

Nathan Hamilton at Egg Box Publishing and Sean Purdy.

Editorial team:

Beatrice Armstrong
Krishan Coupland
Timothy Lawrence
Rachel Mendel
Matthew McGuinness
Faith Ng
Caroline Pearce
Lauren Rose
Naomi Spicer
Jo Surzyn
Laura Westerman

Contents

....

University of East Anglia

Creative Writing Anthologies

2013

3 4114 00674 7801

egg b●x   University of East Anglia

UEA Non-Fiction Anthology 2013

First published by Egg Box Publishing 2013

International © 2013 retained by individual authors

This book is sold subject to the condition that it shall not, by way of trade or otherwise, be lent, resold, hired out, stored in a retrieval system, or otherwise circulated without the publisher's prior consent in any form of binding or cover other than that in which it is published and without a similar condition including this condition being imposed on the subsequent purchaser.

A CIP record for this book is available from the British Library.

UEA Nonfiction Anthology 2013 is typeset in 10pt Caslon with 13pt leading. Titles in Din, of various weights.

Printed and bound in the UK by Imprint Digital.

Designed and typeset by Sean Purdy.

Cover photography by Oliver Balaam.

Proofread by Sarah Gooderson.

Distributed by Central Books.

ISBN: 9780957661134

....

....

Introduction

Kathryn Hughes

This year's non-fiction writers have stayed pretty close to home. Not that there's anything remotely parochial about this collection of bitter-sweet meditations on family life. Dannielle Shaw, for instance, tells us what it's like to have your nan's titled employer turn up at your hospital birth dressed as Minnie Mouse. Alexis Wolf ponders why blackberrying is so crucial to her father's still-emerging sense of Americanness, decades after his parents first put down roots. On the other side of the world, in the foggy streets of 'sixties Islington, Catherine Coldstream recalls a paint-spattered childhood with her father, the distinguished artist William Coldstream.

Of course families can go wrong too, bending themselves into uncanny, even hostile, shapes. Jessica Reik's piece deals with her return to her late grandmother's house, where the refrigerator seems to have taken on a talismanic quality. Julie Osburn tracks the ghosts that come calling down the decades. Naomi Spicer, meanwhile, wants us all to know, really know, that when people die it's not like the movies.

Other people's families are important too. Caroline Pearce explores the story of little Gwen Lack, handed over to Dr Barnardo's in the 1930s. Lynne Harries journeys north in an attempt to plot the girlhood of her late friend, Anna Mendelssohn, better known as the avant-garde poet Grace Lake. Finally Lyndsey Jenkins, roaming furthest, goes to Ghana to bring us the extraordinary story of Paul Apowida, a 'spirit child' who managed, against the murderous odds, to remain safely tethered to the earth.

What all this writing has in common is a fierce determination to imagine the familiar in new and startling ways. This isn't about showy tricks and cheap feeling. Rather, our graduating writers have looked steadily at the world, attended to both its patterns and disruptions, and brought back accounts that make us want to look, and look again.

....

Kathryn Hughes is Director of the MA in Biography and Creative Non-Fiction

Catherine Coldstream

William Coldstream: a Natural History
An extract from a work in progress

I could have started with turpentine. Or with brushes. Rags and jam jars, and murky, paint-dried palettes. Oil and pigment bleeding from twisted tubes onto half a dozen Georgian mantelpieces. Burnt Sienna, Raw Umber, Alizarin Crimson, Titanium White. The sticky-sweet viscosity of linseed oil, the spirit-thin transparency of meths, the little balls of fraying cotton wool we found dotted around the house, each pungent with its own solvent and marked with a different code, a different colour, the DNA of my father's work, the painting which was his life-blood. His art was a form of natural selection. We, his biological children, shared our nurturing with still lifes, nudes, and formal portraits, inhabited a London landscape that was all the greyer for being observed (with all the tools of a painter's unflinching rigor) through tortoiseshell spectacles, or from the dusty windows of Islington and Camden terraced houses.

Or I could have offered whisky as an aperitif, one evoking cloudy crystal tumblers, soda siphons, and the ashtrays that were part of the social equipment of our home (God knows there were few other concessions to relaxation). Or perhaps the whiff of occasional sherry, the Bristol Cream that was trundled out once a year, or the sherry that prevented the Christmas pudd from festering. I might have led you through the darkened Hall into the kitchen, to the smell of burning toast, the clatter of cutlery or the tinkling of the little bronze bell my sister had rigged up, on a string from attic to basement as an alarm.

I could have begun with the rustle of my mother's paisley dresses, or the skipping of her leather sandals, as she danced along to Carmen in the kitchen, the scratch of needle against vinyl as she jostled against the turntable, the clicking of fingers a percussive obbligato. But I am going to begin with hearsay. And with the records of a life begun nearly sixty years before I was born. These at least provide a respectable background, a natural sense of history and of my father's formative years.

A '*sea green incorruptible*', or an '*éminence grise*'[1] – such solemn things have been said about my father, who dressed in grey and chaired committees, and measured out his subjects' lives carefully and by the millimetre, in pigment, solvents, oil, and resin . He did this on rough-stretched canvases in London attics and behind creaking bedroom doors. He did it from the depths of Bloomsbury studios and from the tops of high-rise City buildings. He did it with boiled linseed and in the dingiest of muted shades, excluding vibrancy and warmth. And he did it at arm's length, steadying his brush with a stocky, deliberate thumb, aiming for cool detachment, emotional independence from his sitters. His was a slow, meticulous art, calculated to objectify the human individual, isolating him or her from cumbersome context and environment. Under the rigour of his gaze his subjects were shed of history and personality, exposed, denuded in a thousand careful strokes.

Some were already naked; the young women who would come from Hampstead, Clapham, or the suburbs, undress, and fling themselves happily on horsehair, the surgical chaise longue inherited from a medical father, and sit (or lie) stock still, only the breath between nostril and chest moving, imperceptibly, over hours. I imagine the ticking of a clock, and the erratic bursts of my father's witty interjections, punctuating sessions of high concentration, the silence filled with purposeful intent. A single word from him was like the crackling of a firework, his laughter like the tingling hiss of sparklers on a winter's night. Other sitters were less obviously exposed; the men in flannel, or in tweed or twill, with mortar boards and academic gowns, establishment figures whose portraits hang today in panelled halls. One such subject, noting the arrhythmic shift

....

1 – David Sylvester, 'Grey Eminence', *New Statesman*, 27 March 1962

between banter and cold concentration, said of the latter that, 'it was like looking up suddenly into the aimed barrel of a marksman'.[2]

For all the calculation of his craft, my father was not a chilly personality, but vital, warm, and irreverently witty. Perhaps it was the intensity of feeling that drove him to seek artistic nirvana in complete detachment; sometimes a stark extreme is needed to counteract excess. Or it may have been his ascetic family background; growing up the son of a GP, he was at home in the clinical atmosphere of a Northumbrian (or London) surgery. His friend Wystan Auden, addressing him in 1937, notes this unique combination of watchfulness and warmth, the bid for emotional mastery, shot through with irrepressible wit that revelled in the telling detail.

> 'An artist you said, is both perceiver and teller,
> the spy and the gossip ...
> Very well then, let's start with perceiving,
> Let me pretend that I'm the impersonal eye of the camera ...'[3]

Christopher Isherwood's famous adaptation of the analogy turns it on its head, acknowledging the elusiveness of 'mere' observation, in his Goodbye to Berlin. Of his assemblage of mental images – the 'man shaving at the window opposite, and the woman in the kimono washing her hair'[4] – he acknowledges that 'some day, all this will have to be developed, carefully printed, fixed.' All will be subject to decoding and interpretation. For him, there was no such thing as neutral representation.

Neither do I have the impersonal eye of a camera, nor wish to fix my subject to a two-dimensional surface. The man who painted before breakfast, and wrote reports, and paced the corridors of University College London, wiping oily pigment from his hands,

....

2 – Colin St John Wilson, The Artist at Work, Lund Humphries, 1999, p 11
3 – W H Auden, 'Letter to William Coldstream Esq.' in *Letters From Iceland*, in *Prose Volume 1*, ed. Edward Mendelson, Faber and Faber, 1996, p 344
4 – Christopher Isherwood, Goodbye to Berlin, Hogarth Press, 1939, p 1

was also, for me, the one who wheezed mischievously through his whisky, laughed at me often, until he cried, and liked nothing better than kippers on toast, or family holidays at the seaside. He was an irrepressible lover of cricket and of chess, of poetry, beer, and ballet, and of evenings spent with friends, laughing into the helpless hours. For us, his children, he was first and foremost a magician; under his gaze we lived contented. Apart from him, anxiety reigned.

The 'shilling lives'[5] have been written; they will tell you he was born in 1908, a doctor's son, in Belford, Northumberland, the youngest of five children. They will record the family move to London two years later, and the instability and illness that followed, exempting him from school. The years of home-based education under a private tutor, his obsession with Natural History and drawing (he kept snakes and lizards in the surgery basement, observing and sketching them extensively), would all be noted, as would his admission to the Slade School of Fine Art at University College London, aged eighteen. Then sixty further years, embracing two marriages, five children, a professorship and countless accolades, would be sketched against a foggy London backdrop, together, perhaps, with some sad acknowledgement of his tendency to depression. Not all biographers like to mention the periods of breakdown, one in the early '60s, triggering his impulsive second marriage, the other in the '80s, foreshadowing his death in Bloomsbury, on a snowy February day in 1987. The snowdrops were pushing up in Russell Square that afternoon.

These observations, like my father's work, belong merely to the realm of naked fact (at least, that is what he liked to tell himself, and would certainly have us believe) expunged of all but the slightest commentary. I chose to add the snowdrops and the snakes myself, for fear the account might lose all resemblance to the man, a man deeply attuned to the vibrancy of the natural world, the tender,

....

5 – W H Auden, Who's Who, in Selected Poems, ed Edward Mendelson, Vintage, 1990

quivering potentiality of the passing minute. There were snowdrops in Russell Square as he lay dying, and snakes in his basement as he grew up, a precocious and oversensitive child. Such detail belongs not to the Square as he lay dying, and snakes in his basement as he grew up, a precocious and oversensitive child. Such detail belongs not to the cold obituary, nor to the eye of the impartial camera, but to the battered family album, heavy with associations. It is reminiscent of the photograph itself, one curling at the edges, found in the bowels of a favoured bureau, or of a cloudy family portrait hanging on a further wall. I have a stash of such recollections, images filed roughly but in no particular order, a pointillist array of living moments.

To take a celebrated photograph, however, as a starting point, I ask you to walk back with me, to 1937, and to The Downs School, Malvern, where three men stand squinting into the sun against a garden wall. This trio of male figures, dressed in near identical, loose-fitting suits and posing (playfully, even flamboyantly), are Wystan Auden, Benjamin Britten, and in the centre of the group, my father, his arm outstretched and steadying a plumb line, his eyes narrowed in estimatory intent. Demonstrating the tools of their respective trades, each man holds some object for the viewer to decode: the poet a several-times folded sheet of paper, one long and broad enough for a dozen stanzas, from which he appears to be reading, lost in thought. The musician holds a smaller sheet, presumably of manuscript, from which he looks up smiling, both coy and eager, as though about to sing, or to address a friendly audience. The painter alone gazes into the middle distance, intent on measurements, utterly focused on his goal. He is the clinical observer, the empiricist, Britten the performer, and Auden the contemplative, quietly assessing human nature. Together they stand self-consciously as the Three Graces, enjoying each other's company as much as the art forms they aspire to embody.

The image is rich not only in symbolism, and in high theatricality and style, but also in the specifics of a shared history, a seminal time in the lives of three young men and rooted, as the photograph suggests, in a sunny day in June. The setting was Auden's territory; aged thirty at this point, he had taught English at The Downs for over three years, composing his 'Vision of Agape' while there. Britten (then only twenty-four) and my father (twenty-nine) are present too, not merely as visiting teachers at the school, but as friends and collaborators, who worked closely with Auden at the GPO Film Unit, making documentaries under John Grierson. At the time this image was taken things were already coming to a head; Auden was soon to withdraw from the Unit following a row with producer Basil Wright, and my father and Britten to follow, in disappointment at the artistic limitations imposed by a narrowly industrial, or impersonal agenda.

Their own disillusionment had taken them by surprise. They had gone in with high intent, with ideals of 'social relevance' and a deep-seated discomfort with the elitism they perceived as afflicting the arts. Only three years later, however, Auden was able to write to Lawrence Gowing, one of his most promising students: 'you want to get into film because you think it is the art of the future; it isn't. Art is the art of the future.'[6] The three young men, squinting into the sun against that garden wall, had both individually and collectively reached the same position by the summer of 1937. While 'documentation' would remain important to all three, in the sense that each was committed to a clear-eyed representation of the everyday in art, Documentary, as such, was over for them.

....

6 – Lawrence Gowing, Remembering Coldstream, Tate Gallery, 1990, p 9

William Coldstream: a Natural History

© Unknown photographer, 1937. Image reproduced courtesy of the Britten–Pears Foundation (www.brittenpears.org) Ref: PH/4/57. Title: 'W H Auden, William Coldstream and Benjamin Britten outside The Downs School, Colwall, posing as the Three Graces', June 1937.

....

Catherine Coldstream was born in London in 1962, and is an Oxford-based teacher and musician, with a background in theology. She has written a memoir, *The Effects of Turpentine and Other Spirits*, and is working on the first draft of a novel. Her book about her father is a hybrid piece that blends biography, memory and reflection.

Lynne Harries

Who we were, where we were
An extract

This is from an attempt to catch memories of the poet Anna Mendelssohn through 'place' – Cambridge was my town from 1972. She arrived in 1983 and stayed until her death in 2009: never settled; never out of the orbit of the University Library.

2003

W e had not considered the impact of Valentine's Day on our trip until we set out to look for supper. Neither of us had visited the town before, though Simon must have driven nearby, on business. Among the many northern towns I did not know, it had identified itself as a picturesque setting for tales of the supernatural and the country residences of Premiership footballers and their families.

The hotel was ideal – everybody occupied with a big wedding party. We walked up and down the main street – it was already dark – and got a table at a small bistro.

So we came, twenty–five years married, to be sitting at a tiny table with pink cloth scattered with sharp confetti hearts, drinking Seaview rosé and eating lamb cutlets and strawberry tarts.

The bedroom was overheated; we had stuffed our Marks and Spencer sandwiches into the minibar and loaded the van with bottled water. There was nothing to do but to try to sleep. The next morning, we found the Edge, and walked for as long as we could bear. We didn't know what lay ahead but were both guessing, in silence, waiting for the call.

The house was where it should be, twenty miles away, in a quiet cul-de-sac. Now that I visit the north often, I am familiar with the layout of the large, once-prosperous towns: the grand civic centre with its pound shops and arts initiatives; the miles of discount tile sheds and carpet warehouses; the good and less good suburbs.

Anna had spoken more about her parents in recent years. She was talkative about details that I would guess she had once repressed – a quick-thinking girl on a one-way ticket out of Stockport. Now she was glad to be back in the shelter of the house she had been born in, orphaned on the threshold of old age, exclaiming over the conveniences of the pebbledashed 1930s house, in its double corner plot.

Over the last year, she had supervised the correct mourning of her parents, who had died within a month of each other: the funeral and yahrzeit, planting memorial trees at the cemetery. There was no congregation in Stockport now, where once every market stall, every tailor and upholsterer, had been a Jewish business supporting a son or daughter studying law or medicine. Religious life had been absorbed into the Greater Manchester area. Her parents, though, were buried under the black mulberry and sweet almond, near their own parents: the ones who had walked the triangle from Liverpool to Manchester to Leeds, looking for work, off the onion boat.

The board went up in the garden, the house was sold. Anna's sister Judy, who had the silver candlesticks even though she was the younger daughter, was waiting for the transfer of half the funds to her bank account, at home in The Hague. Anna was planning to return, with our help, to the unheated garden building – the studio, she called it, or *le kiosque du jardin* – bringing most of the moveable possessions of her parents' and grandparents' hundred-year sojourn in this land.

Back in the early years of the twenty-first century, Anna had prepared us lunch. Little cartons of hummus and olives, bought from Farhid at the deli who had wept to hear she was leaving, were balanced along the mantelpiece in the sitting room. She wanted to talk, to have coffee. Lustre cups sat unpacked for this, and Italian biscuits on a plate.

In fact, most things were unpacked. Writings and paintings seemed to have received some attention: a scree or floe across the floor, dividing and clumping along not-obvious lines. She had stacked framed certificates against the wall: her Aunt Estelle's savings had caused a hundred trees to be planted in Israel; the synagogue committee wished her grandparents naches on the occasion of their fiftieth wedding anniversary; Anne Mendleson was awarded the gold medal for elocution and verse speaking.

We left the huge box that was the television with its bottle-glass screen; she was angry that we couldn't take the 1950s kitchen fittings, banging them hard with the flat of her hand. A neighbour, Howard, came and helped Simon to load the van. Howard and June, a couple in their forties, were sorry to see Anna go and promised to stay in touch. She remembered each of them as children. There were possibly old people here who remembered her as a child; certainly everyone now resident in 'the Grove' had known her parents through their long retirement. Howard took a screwdriver and freed the plaque with the number of her ancestral home, nine, and she climbed into the cab and carried it off on her knee.

1972

When I arrived here as a student, Cambridge was very small – small like a quiet market town with a university attached, smaller in the number of students, and much smaller in the extent of their need or desire to stray from the orbit of the colleges, their bars and dining halls, and the city centre shops where you could buy a Mars bar, cigarettes, a newspaper, books of course, an occasional item of clothing (literally occasional in the sense of the highly specific outfits required for college sports and dining clubs) and, from Mrs Hunt on Magdalene Street, outside the now unimaginably limited trading hours, one egg or two ounces of butter. Students biked about zestfully enough, especially those who actually attended morning lectures, and the athletes and rowers; in the summer you might cycle to a pub in Coton or Dry Drayton or Newton, or picnic in a cornfield behind the

University Library (though the most popular destination was surely anywhere on the Cam or Granta, especially Grantchester, by punt). Girton College represented the far north; the lock at Jesus Green the east, a little further from the 'colonies' of second year students but not as far as the obvious civilian division of the Mitcham's corner one-way system (the boathouses after all could be more conveniently reached by cycling across Jesus Green and along the Midsummer Common towpath). Methodists might find the Wesley Church, Quakers the Park Street Meeting House and Roman Catholics the Church of Our Lady and the English Martyrs on Hills Road, a landmark bus stop and a cue that you were on the right road for the railway station – though the last group might favour the Fisher House Chaplaincy, tucked behind Petty Cury, off the market square. You would hit the centre coming from the east at the edge of Parker's Piece and, catching a train, Mass or Fenners permitting, you would turn back from the south and up to the western quarter of the circle, past the science buildings on Lensfield Road. If you were very specifically drawn to the engineering building, the architecture faculty, the Fitzwilliam or Peterhouse's new high-rise accommodation, you could approach the central precincts of Little St Mary's, Pembroke, Silver Street and Great St Mary's from there. Beyond the Backs, the University Library must surely have been a conclusive boundary for everyone except members of the University Real Tennis Club, just behind in Grange Road. Visits to Newnham College or to research students' houses for supervisions, to the West Road faculty buildings and concert hall might be frequent but these trajectories radiated out from the centre or strung themselves across its spokes, like the connecting strands of a spider's web.

This was my world: I had entered it on the same terms as Anna, when she went to the University of Essex at Wivenhoe, near Colchester: that is to say, temporarily, as a reward for years of solitary study, and conditionally, subject to good behaviour. Anna's career at Essex was already over when mine was starting in Cambridge. We did not know each other, or know that we had mutual friends. She did not have the opportunity to see my likeness in the newspapers and on television, as I did hers.

When we met in 1983, I was living at the far end of Chesterton Road, an area that would have been outside my scope ten years before, were it not that my college owned a block of Art Deco-style flats almost opposite. These were let to graduate students and college staff – I had occupied one for some months in 1975. Through the agency of her sponsor in Clare, the Fellow who was helping her to apply for a place as an undergraduate next autumn, Anna had been given a flat there with room for her three year old and the baby that she was expecting. As my former Director of Studies and now my employer, he introduced us to each other with the idea of reading French together for her entrance exam. We didn't bump pushchairs in the street though, given our proximity, we were pretty well mutually ineluctable. For a long time now, my Cambridge had been criss-crossed by other tracks: to nursery school and primary school; doctor, nurse and dentist; swimming classes, music lessons, the swings. Anna in her turn discovered the walk along the Backs to the University Library and lingered in the cafés behind King's Parade.

EKPHRASIS

There may be lots of these: the smallest feature of the landscape that acts as a spur to memory, the things we leave behind. This is a top item, a self-proclaimed memento; not the most poignant but one for the public.

A ten inch stemmed glass, not hand-made, but engraved by hand:

I have never heard of anyone walking
right through another's work in progress
nor smashing it and kicking the paintress
through her composition albeit that the waves
do not stay still for her albeit that she is not
stretched over her canvas as it rafts her out to sea
to be dashed against the headland which was
so internally unpeopled eternally exempt

from broken skulls forming
the jagged centre of a split morphology.

FROZEN MOMENTS   I.M. Joan Eardley

Grace Lake

I have transcribed this as accurately as possible with regard to the layout on the curved surface of the glass.

I was with Anna the day this was presented to her: a day in early September, because I was just back from Scotland and every year, as late as possible into August, our family went there on holiday. We were meeting at the Café Rouge near St John's. Anna was with the parents of a young man called Gibson, who admired her work. She must have met him in the library or a poetry event – less likely, as she was shy at the latter and often bolted. His mother had engraved the glass with a poem supplied by Anna, and now it was ready. The subject, Joan Eardley, was a kind of cult with us; we seemed to discover her painting at about the same time (prompted I think by a retrospective in 1990) and Anna was the first to send me a postcard of her work. As a regular visitor to Scotland, I was more likely to see it though, over the years, and to visit Catterline, the fishing village on the East Coast, the site of all her late landscapes, and where she died in 1962. I became the source of catalogues and postcards – though we had an afternoon together at the Mercury Gallery in Cork Street, grandly letting the assistants bring up canvas after canvas – and of the round pebbles that had rolled across the North Sea from Norway.

....

Lynne Harries is writing a memoir of her friendship with the poet Anna Mendelssohn. She lives in Cambridge and is particularly interested in writing about the poetry and visual arts of the Modernist movement.

Lyndsey Jenkins

Spirit Boy

Paul Apowida is running home, towards the men who tried to kill him.

He runs east towards the sun along the steaming tarmac on the road out from Bolgatanga towards Navrongo in Northern Ghana. On the approach to the tiny village of Sirigu, the dirt road is almost completely flat. The single hill stands sharply against the skyline as Paul runs past. His breathing is ragged and his T-shirt is soaking.

Today, this hill is a place where men go to survey their millet crops. But ten years ago, it was scattered with skulls.

These were the broken bones of the *kinkuru*: the spirit children.

A child was killed nearly every day and left out on the hillside to rot. Twenty-five years ago the men who killed those babies came for Paul.

Before Paul was five years old, they had tried to murder him twice. He barely survived the poisoning. They would inevitably try again, so Paul was smuggled away in the middle of the night to an orphanage hundreds of miles away. For his own safety, Paul was kept away from his brothers, his village and his clan. He grew up an outsider as well as an orphan.

Paul is twenty-seven now, an artist and a soldier. He is running a marathon to raise money for AfriKids, the British charity which saved his life, put him through art school and helped him join the British Army.

He is also the rarest of creatures: a living spirit boy.

Paul runs at least six miles each day, but the wet fields outside Chepstow were poor training for this intense heat. Paul is led by two professional athletes and trailed by an AfriKids jeep. Outside Sirigu, crowds have gathered to welcome this famous son of the village home.

Today, Paul will stand up in front of the family who wanted him dead and the child-killers who were prepared to murder him, a living testament to what spirit children can be. AfriKids has worked in Sirigu for over a decade to combat the deadly belief in spirit children. Now, as a result of their efforts and Paul's example, his community and his people will renounce their ancient tradition and pledge that no more spirit children will be killed.

*

Paul Apowida was born in 1985, the fourth child and third son of an important man in the community. In a society where wealth is measured in pots and wives, this family was well off. But life in Sirigu is precarious and fragile even for the richest of families. One day when Paul was about three months old, his mother headed to the market to trade for tobacco, salt and rice. Between the busy stalls, the ground swayed beneath her eyes. She turned her head and vomited, right in the middle of the market square. A woman squealed. Paul's mother collapsed. She was dead within a few minutes.

Back at home, Paul's grandmother, taking care of Paul, his sister and brothers, under the shade of a tree, was already feeling unwell. Out building a new mud hut, his father felt nauseous and came down the ladder, only to collapse at the bottom. In the millet fields, his cousins found shelter and lay down to rest, wondering if the unusual heat was affecting them. By the end of the day, eight members of Paul's family were dead.

The official cause of death was meningitis, but Paul's family knew better. How could all those healthy, strong adults have died when this tiny baby had survived?

The answer was obvious. Paul must be a spirit child.

In Sirigu, as in many places across Africa, the spirit world hovers just out of reach. Dead ancestors are as present and real as living relatives, and soothsayers run a brisk trade mediating between the living and the dead. The soothsayers not only foretell the future, they can change it by warning of danger or advising on a course of action. But ancestors aren't always kind and helpful. If a family fails to pay the ancestors enough attention or honour, they may be sent a spirit child as punishment. That spells disaster.

A spirit child is a malicious demon, intent on causing trouble. Spirit children have incredible powers, able to kill or injure, bring bad luck or ill health, or drain away the family fortune. As long as they live, a spirit child will cause nothing but grief and anguish for the family. The spirit child does not belong in this world. It hates and fears the living as much as it is hated and feared. So it must be sent back to the ancestors. The threat must be destroyed before the threat destroys the family.

Spirit children come in many forms. Some are easy to spot, especially those with deformities or disabilities. These are very common in Ghana, because few pregnant women will regularly see midwives. Most of these children will die anyway. But many cases are less obvious. Ugly babies, babies with large heads or small limbs, babies who cry all night or stare into their mothers' eyes while feeding – any or all of these babies might be accused of being spirit children. In many cases, there are simple medical explanations for their appearance or their behaviour. But explanations aren't as powerful as superstitions.

The belief in spirit children is not unique to Sirigu, or even to Ghana. It is a belief that takes many different forms, with different names, all across Africa and around the world. These days though, it is a largely rural phenomenon, in areas with desperate poverty and deeply held superstitions. In the cities, where the people have healthcare and education, they don't need to believe in spirit children, because there are fewer problems and more answers.

Some communities throw out their spirit children and abandon them to their fate on the street. Some lock their spirit children up so they can't cause any damage. The parents push food under the door and hurry away before they can be contaminated. These spirit children could live for years without seeing another human being.

Some communities perform something like an exorcism, sprinkling medicine around the house to draw the spirit out. But in Sirigu, the solution is quick and simple. The children are killed and then not spoken of again.

The spirit child phenomenon is difficult to explain and easy to judge. It is an ancient and powerful belief, but it is more than just voodoo and witchcraft. It is the product of a poverty which is almost beyond comprehension. The people of Sirigu work day and night yet still barely have enough to feed themselves. If they have a child without legs, they cannot take care of the child. If the mother dies, the father cannot feed the baby. If they have a child who cries all night, they cannot farm during the day. In these circumstances, when the child will probably die anyway, when feeding that child takes precious food away from other children, parents may see killing that child as the pragmatic, sensible – even merciful – thing to do.

The belief in spirit children also has complicated links with power in this ancient and traditional society. Women share the general belief in spirit children, but are less likely to believe that a child they have carried in their own bodies is a demon. But their opinion doesn't count. They aren't even consulted. The men, uninvolved in the intimate details of their babies' lives, make dispassionate decisions about who lives and who dies.

*

Paul's uncle was now the head of the family. He gathered the men of the family together for a conference and shared out pito, the local alcohol, as he listened to the shouts of fear. The conversation was brief because the evidence was overwhelming. Paul was clearly a spirit child. So Paul's uncle went in search of the concoction man.

Ghana's concoction men have been called by the gods to protect their people. They perform a vital service, keeping the community safe from demons. They are well paid for their work, proud of their role, and fanatical in their commitment to ridding the world of suspected spirits. Every village has several concoction men, each vigilant and alert to any potential threats. Fathers teach their sons their mysterious rites: how to interpret signals from the ancestors and how to brew the secret poison from roots and herbs. No one else knows the recipe, which has been blended to deadly perfection after generations of practice. It is a serious business and a huge responsibility. One mistake may mean a spirit child is free to bring destruction to an entire village.

The poison is very strong. Lots of children die instantly. Others will take a few minutes. Some children survive the poison but die of exposure in the intense heat. A few survive. This is a dilemma for the family. Some will rejoice and welcome the baby back into the family. Others will be afraid this spirit must be particularly vicious and nasty. In these cases, there is nothing left to do but attack the baby, hitting or strangling him until he is dead. Then the remains will be cast out onto the hill. There will be no ceremony, no burial. Just relief. The family moves on, as if the child never lived.

*

Paul's uncle brought the concoction man back to the compound where he could examine the infant. He held Paul at a distance: scrutinising him almost scientifically, before beginning his ritual. The women were shooed away. The concoction man took a black and white chicken and held it squawking into the sky. His left hand tightened around the chicken's scrawny neck and his right hand took a long brown knife, almost like a dagger. He sawed at the chicken's throat. The family stood back, watching and waiting. The concoction man turned the chicken upside down, allowing the blood to drip down onto the ground below. Then he threw it, almost casually, onto the ground. It flapped and squawked, then lay still. The wings were broken backwards, the feathers pointing upwards to the skies.

The concoction man whooped. This was a clear signal from the ancestors. Without doubt, Paul must be a spirit. He leapt around the chicken's body, smearing his feet in blood, to thank the ancestors. After that, there was no time to waste. Watching Paul intently, careful in case the demon realised what was happening and tried to strike, he took out his pouch full of poisonous herbs. He grabbed the baby by the hair and forced his head back so he could stuff the toxic mixture into Paul's mouth. Then the concoction man held Paul's arms tightly for a few minutes while he struggled, making sure he didn't spit the herbs out, or throw them up. The poison is fast acting. It didn't take long until Paul gave up his protests and lay limp and pathetic. Then he was thrown out of the compound like trash, left to lie naked under the blazing sun. His family stood around, shuffling their feet, muttering to each other, and waiting for Paul to die.

Lyndsey Jenkins has been a speechwriter for five cabinet ministers. She is interested in feminism, politics, writers and particularly the lives of pioneering and creative women from the early twentieth century. Her dissertation is on Constance Bulwer-Lytton, an upper-class suffragette who disguised herself as working class to experience the hunger strikes. *Spirit Boy*, written with Paul Apowida, will be published by Silvertail Books in 2013.

Julie Osburn

Ghosts

1970

'**S**low down!'

Mike has his foot to the floor, speeding his pale green 1965 Chevrolet Impala Coupe up Bellaire Boulevard so fast that when we reach the top of the hill, he barely brakes in time for the four-way stop.

'Shut up. Who's driving?'

'You are.'

'And if you tell Mom I'm speeding what'll happen?'

'I won't get rides.'

'Right. So shut up.'

Mike drops me off in front of the theatre, pulling his car to the kerb with a jerk. 'Have fun. Don't scare the ghosts.'

'Shut up, Mike! I told you that in secret!'

'Don't slam the door,' he yells as I slam it. He peels away, rushing to his job at O'Leary's Ice Cream Parlour where he performs magic tricks and serves floats and boats with blue sugar cube flames.

I run through the double glass doors clutching my script. 'Sorry I'm late! My *brother* had to drive me.' Leanne turns around with her finger to her mouth. Rehearsal's already started. Leanne was my teacher at Casa Mañana Acting School. My first monologue in class was Emily's end speech when she was a ghost in *Our Town*. I cried and people clapped so I'm pretty much hooked for life. Leanne invited me into this acting workshop for teens sponsored by Texas Christian University. She says even though I'm young I have what it takes.

We're rehearsing *Pegora The Witch*. It's my first role on a real stage. I'm going to leave Texas and be a big star, even if I start out as just the Assistant Witch in a kids' play.

I shrug apologetically to Leanne for interrupting rehearsal and sit next to my new best friend Anson. He points down to the Ouija board sticking out of his backpack on the floor between his legs. We suck in our lips in anticipation of our lunch break in the basement. We're the youngest in the workshop. Anson's twelve and short and still a kid. I'm twelve and three-quarters and five foot seven which makes me old enough and tall enough to be taught how to French kiss in a game of spin the bottle by Peter, the oldest in the workshop. He's the handsomest nineteen-year-old boy-man who ever gave me the time of day. And to top it all off he has a goatee and moustache.

Peter told us The Little Theatre where we hold rehearsals and performances is haunted. It has a dark refrigerator-cold basement used for dressing rooms and storing props. Anson and I use it for séances, Ouija boards, and ghost stories. During lunch break we go downstairs to hide in the darkest, coldest corner of the haunted basement.

Anson's Parker Brothers Ouija Board comes in a game box just like *Chutes and Ladders* or *Monopoly*. The board looks like it was designed hundreds of years ago with ink drawings of the sun and moon, a Victorian lady with her hand on a planchette, and a ghost's head floating behind her, whispering in her ear. It has a YES in the upper left corner with the sun and NO in the upper right with the moon. The alphabet is in two rows, arched in a double rainbow. Numbers from 0-9 are below in a straight line. At the very bottom it says GOODBYE.

Anson says it's simple. You put two fingers each on the planchette, ask the board a question and let the ghost move the planchette. If you move it yourself you're cheating. Ghosts can answer yes or no, they can write words or numbers. Most important: you must make the ghosts say GOODBYE or they can possess you, haunting you forever. We put our fingers on the planchette, trying to call up the spirit of my grandfather Osburn. I never met him because he died when Dad was only eighteen, but since he was family he might be hanging around.

I call out his name, 'Charles Osburn? Are you there?' The planchette is still on the board. Not even a wiggle. 'I am looking for Charles Osburn. Are you there?' The planchette glides to the sun. YES, it says. My body jolts, electrified with nerves. I look suspiciously at Anson.

'I didn't move it!' He spurts saliva down his chin. The planchette moves back to the centre. Anson whispers so softly I have to read his lips in the dimmed light. 'Try it again. Ask it something else.'

'Are you my grandfather?' YES says the board. 'Are you sure?' YES says the board. 'Can you spell your last name?' Nobody spells it right.

The planchette hesitates before sliding to the first letter: F. Osburn doesn't begin with F. The planchette moves to the second letter. U. The beats in my chest are racing to escape my body. I can even feel them in my legs and toes. Who is this spirit? The next letter. C. 'Who are you?' I practically expect the last K when it comes. There is menace in the basement. The walls, the floor, even the air grows hard and closes in around me, pressing on my skull. 'You are not my grandfather. You can't spell Osburn! You're a liar!!!' The planchette goes wild, circling the board three times before flying across the room. It hits a wall and clatters to the floor. Too scared to scream, Anson and I simultaneously leap to our feet and run upstairs two at a time to the grey light of an empty stage where more ghosts lurk in dark corners. I step centre stage, protected in the safe zone. I decide theatre ghosts are dead actors to help me become a star, but basement ghosts are only dead crew members and acting wannabes. Basement ghosts kick us out of our bodies to come back to life. That lying spirit didn't say GOODBYE. That spirit could follow me home and take over my body and haunt me forever.

A week later and figuring there's safety in numbers, Anson and I assemble a larger group in the theatre basement in a corner between the stored flats and discarded props and sit cross-legged in a circle on the concrete floor. Harriet, the Head Witch, turns off the light. I sit with my back to the wall so the lying spirit can't strangle me from behind. We breathe lightly, listening for any ghosts who might be prowling in the cold dusty air. I act cool. I don't want anybody to think I'm a wimp.

Peter, my boy-man with the sexy goatee takes the flashlight and holds it under his chin making his cheekbones bright bluish white, his eyes big black holes. He croons in soft bass about a faraway land called Devon over a hundred years ago.

'There was a brother and sister who loved each other so much they couldn't stand to be apart, but it was time for them to grow up and forge their own lives.'

I dive into the deep end of his smoky voice, imagining Mike and me in Devon in long skirts and tails and wild flowing hair. I imagine loving Mike that much. This takes some work since most of the time I hate him because most of the time he socks me in the arm and says 'Does that hurt?' until I cry.

'The girl made her brother promise that if one of them died, their spirit would visit the other to say goodbye.'

A gust of freezing air blows down on us. Anson yells 'BOO!' and we all jump out of our gourds and scream. Anson laughs at us and we laugh back, but Peter sits still with the flashlight on his face, waiting like the devil himself until we fall again under his spell. I close my eyes because I keep seeing shadows moving across the far wall.

'One night as the clock struck twelve, the sister woke up from a cold wind blowing across her eyes. Standing at the foot of her bed was her brother. "No!" she said. "Please tell me you're OK!" He put his finger to his lips. "I kept my vow," he said, then vanished. It was a vow she knew was a curse. Her brother was dead.'

1972

All My Children is on. I am lying on the floor at the foot of my bed, two feet in front of my nineteen inch black and white TV. My favourite characters are in love, but just as Mary's about to confess this huge secret that she's actually a nun, Mike storms into my room without knocking and throws himself on my bed with his guitar.

'Listen to this song I just wrote for Nancy. It's really cool.'

'Get out of my room! *All My Children* is on!!!!'

He narrows his eyes and juts his lower jaw out at me like I'm the stupidest person on the planet. 'That's a soap. It's soap crap.' He caresses his beat-up twelve string. 'This is music. This is art. This is love.'

'I don't care about your girlfriend or your song! This is my room! I don't want you here! Get out of here! Get out!'

He stands up, acting disgusted at me, which makes me hate him more. He storms back to the door. 'Fine. But you just lost your only chance to hear the best song I ever wrote.' He slams the door behind him so hard my full-length poster of Paul Newman shudders in his wake.

I turn up the volume to the TV and settle back to my position on the blue and green shag carpet.

A clear voice that is not my own, not a fleeting thought, nor a pang of guilt, but a clear voice inside my head instructs me firmly, 'Turn off the TV. Go into his room. Tell him you're sorry. Listen to his song. Do it now.' The instruction is so urgent and strong, the voice so present I know I must do as it says. I turn off the TV, knock at Mike's door, and wait for him to say 'Come in.' I tell him I'm sorry. I'd like to hear his song.

He shrugs easily. Pleased.

'OK.' He even smiles at me.

I curl into Ma B's old hand-me-down rocker and listen to 'NanC's Song.' It's good. I don't even mind when he sings off key.

It's been a whole day since I sat in the rocker and listened to Mike play his song. There are too many people at the house. Too many people who tell me they know how I feel. Too many Frito Lay Casseroles and Bundt cakes and homemade fried chicken. Ma B says that's what Texas folk do. They bring food so we'll eat instead of weep. But Mom can't stop crying. She may never stop.

I escape the house, breathing in warm spring air with yellow-gold sun on my face. The cicadas whine their late afternoon song in the trees. They're early this year, which means a hot summer coming. I walk along the creek to find the tree, four blocks from our house. We were told he crashed somewhere along Overton Park East, across from the 'Pepto-Bismol-Pink' house. It's easy to find. The forlorn oak stands alone between the road and the creek. Its branches lean left in an upward plea, missing its natural balance. Fifteen inches to either side, his pale green 1965 Chevrolet Impala Coupe could have rolled down the gentle bank to the creek. He could've walked home. I run my hand over the fresh gash where his car hit. Someone's carved his name in the trunk. Blood rushes to my cheeks. If you're going to carve a boy's name into the tree that killed him, shouldn't you spell it right?

'It's only a name, Julie. Doesn't matter how it's spelled.' Mike's behind me, whispering in my ear. 'Don't tell Mom about the tree. She shouldn't see it. Our secret.'

'You didn't say goodbye.'

'You wouldn't let me.'

Julie Osburn developed a love for words while starring on stage (including the West End), TV (including a soap), and silver screen. She finally left Hollywood's gritty glitter to settle in Cambridgeshire and write full time. She is currently writing a memoir and a historical novel on a Tudor hero gone bad.

Caroline Pearce

A True Family
Gwen's story

April 6ᵗʰ 1931 was Gwendoline Ethel Lack's third birthday. What should have been a day of celebration for the round-faced, blonde-haired toddler to enjoy with her family became a day of mourning: at St Mary's Hospital, Highgate, Gwen's father died of bronchial pneumonia. As well as leaving Gwen's mother, Dolly, a widow for a second time, forty-five-year-old Edward Lack's death had profound implications for the poverty-stricken family, setting in motion events whose memories still provoke Gwen's tears more than eighty years later. As Dolly struggled to maintain family life in desperate and challenging circumstances, a weighty decision was taken: to send young Gwen and three of her siblings to a Dr Barnardo's children's home. From there, they were separated and fostered – or 'boarded out' as the process was then known – with families in a Suffolk village. After eleven years, during which contact between them was minimal, Dolly retrieved Gwen from Dr Barnardo's care, taking her back to wartime London. Gwen was sad, confused and angry, resenting what she perceived as Dolly's mercenary action in reclaiming her only when she became old enough to work. But how far were Dolly's actions dictated by Dr Barnardo's and its stringent policies of severance?

*

A grocer by trade – and a widower with two children when he married Dolly – Edward's foresight in taking out a life insurance policy helped alleviate the family's immediate material needs. But the £86 paid out upon his death was soon used up. With eight dependent children and limited financial means, Dolly found herself overwhelmed: the grief of losing another husband, the hardship of managing daily expenses in a country still recovering from the economic wounds of World War I, and the physical demands of caring for so many children were all too much. Unable to earn an income, and with only a minimal widow's pension, Dolly was urged by friends at her Seventh Day Adventist church to send some of her children into the care of Dr Barnardo's, a Christian charity set up to help the 'neglected, forgotten and abused children of east London'.[1] Consequently, three months after Edward's death, Dolly handed Gwen – along with her sister Helen and brothers Raymond and Leslie – to a travelling matron who accompanied them to the Ever Open Door, the Dr Barnardo's children's home in Stepney which acted as a clearing house. The admission document dated July 8th 1931 reports the children were 'clever and good', 'attended Chapel regularly', and 'the Pastor spoke well of them'. All were 'in very good health, were bright and intelligent, well-behaved and of clean habits', so it appeared they were thriving under their mother's care, and did not match the usual profile of charity children. All four children were 'granted admission on the transference of their pension allowance'[2], so when Dolly relinquished their care, her scant income was reduced further. Desperate as she was, it is possible that Dolly was not fully aware of the implications of her actions, or of Dr Barnardo's firm belief in the importance and advantages of severance. Prior to the Children's Act of 1948, parents consigning their children to a charity's care were usually forced to cede all further rights to them, considered a fair exchange for the shelter, food, clothes and education it provided. High unemployment during the Depression of the 1930s meant increasing numbers of middle-class children became seriously impoverished. Nevertheless,

....

1 – Barnardo's website
2 – Barnardo's admission document, 8th July 1931.

as Dolly edged into poverty by circumstance, giving up her children in this manner could have felt like the best of a limited number of unpalatable options and may have brought her as much shame as relief.

The Ever Open Door, Stepney Causeway

Gwen, aged three, the day she arrived at the Ever Open Door

Gwen does not recall leaving her mother and four siblings that summer's day but remembers drinking thick cocoa from chipped enamel mugs at the Ever Open Door. More significantly she recalls the panic she felt and 'my desperate crying in dread of being parted from Helen'. Six years Gwen's senior, Helen was 'more like a mother than my mother was to me and I clung to her with the hope that we could stay together'.[3] Her fear was not unfounded: it was common practice to send siblings to separate foster homes or even overseas where they could be cut off from all contact with their families indefinitely.[4] Thomas Barnardo's chief aim was to situate needy children with respectable hardworking country families who would provide them with 'clean houses', and 'a new and healthy environment' of which a 'true and religious life' was an indispensible part. Contrary to prevailing scientific thought at the time of the eugenics debate, Barnardo believed that if poor children could be 'removed from

....

3 – Interview with Gwen, December 2010
4 – By 1939 Barnardo's alone had shipped almost 30,000 children to Canada. Fewer than 3,000 children were sent to Australia, Fletcher, p71

A True Family

their surroundings early enough and could be kept sufficiently long under training, heredity counts for little, and environment counts for everything.'[5] Equally, according to the Plymouth Brethren – of whom Barnardo was a follower – 'rescuing' children from privation was considered an urgent religious imperative, a necessary step in saving their souls from a life of crime; the Second Coming of Jesus Christ was believed imminent and spiritual salvation needed to take place in advance.[6] Under Dr Barnardo's policy of severance, family contact was actively discouraged; indeed parents were deterred from maintaining any links whatsoever to their children. Viewing their own personal records was not permitted, so children had no means of ascertaining information about their background. Instead, they were taught to see Dr Barnardo's as their 'true family.'[7]

As it turned out, Gwen had no need to be afraid, at least in the short term. Within two weeks of arriving at the Ever Open Door, she and Helen were taken by train to Old Newton, a small village in rural Suffolk where they were introduced to a childless, middle-aged, kindly-looking couple, Maud and George Grimsey.[8] The Grimseys, they were told, were to be their parents and the girls were instructed to call these strangers 'Mum' and 'Dad'. Dr Barnardo's paid Gwen's new parents five shillings a week per child, considered an attractive financial reward at the time, though the organisation emphasised that foster families must not be motivated 'by the greed of gain'.[9] The Grimseys' house was small, an ordinary two-up, two-down, with an outside toilet and no heating or running water. 'It was so chilly in winter', remembers Gwen, 'that ice would often form on the inside of the bedroom windows.' At sixpence a tube toothpaste was considered an unaffordable luxury so Gwen and Helen cleaned their teeth with salt. Life was hard, says Gwen, but 'Mum and Dad Grimsey were fair,

....

5 – Parker, pp15-16
6 – Rose, p30
7 – Barnardo's website
8 – Gwen's two brothers were fostered elsewhere.
9 – Barnardo's website

Mum & Dad Grimsey

firm and kind in the hope that we would grow into decent, honest citizens. They brought us up as if we were their flesh and blood'.[10]

In 1936, after five years with the Grimseys, Helen was reclaimed by her mother. This was permissible under Dr Barnardo's rules allowing children aged fourteen to return to their birth parents on condition that employment had been secured for them. 'I was heartbroken to lose Helen', Gwen recalls, her eyes welling up with tears, even more than seven decades later. 'The situation was completely out of our control. Helen didn't want to leave, and we didn't want her to go, but there was absolutely nothing we could do'.[11] Indeed, foster parents were required by Dr Barnardo's to sign an agreement including a clause committing to 'restore said child to any person sent by [Dr Barnardo's] to receive it, on getting one fortnight's notice of removal'.[12] The Grimseys were powerless to prevent the loss of a child

....

10 – Interview with Gwen, December 2010
11 – Fostered children are never legally 'owned' by those who foster them, who therefore have no legal rights over the children in their care, Fletcher, p24
12 – Rose, p114

A True Family

they had nurtured and loved as if she were their own. Helen wrote letters to Gwen on a regular powerless to prevent the loss of a child they had nurtured and loved as if she were their own. Helen wrote letters to Gwen on a regular basis, though strict rules meant all correspondence went via Barnardo's Director to be scrutinized and edited before being passed on.[13]

Severance policies were applied irrespective of parents' fitness to care for their children. Home visits were rarely authorised and Dr Barnardo's tended to behave as if all its charges were the victims of unworthy parents. Even if parents' circumstances improved, they were seen as exploitative if they tried to reclaim any child reaching employable age. The longer a child stayed in care, the more likely it became that parents were dismissed as uncaring and incompetent. To what extent this approach influenced the youngsters' view of their parents can only be imagined. In any event, the barrier of distance limited many who could not afford to travel even from one side of a city to the other, let alone out to the countryside to see their children. Dr Barnardo's records show that between 1939 and 1942 the only letters or visits Gwen received were from her sister Helen. During the eleven years Gwen was fostered, Dolly visited just three times.

In the spring of 1942, as Gwen's fourteenth birthday approached, she became anxious and afraid that, like Helen, she too would be forced to leave her Suffolk foster family and live with Dolly in bomb-scarred London. Her worries were well founded. The Grimseys had no legal right to object when notice was duly received that Gwen was to be removed from their care. But instead of being returned to Dolly as she had expected, Gwen was taken to Warlies, a Barnardo's-owned residential domestic training centre for girls in Waltham Abbey, Essex. The young residents, known as 'inmates', were mostly girls who were 'certified as mentally defective', 'crippled', and 'unfit' on account of their mentality to take up normal life and work', none of which applied to Gwen, who was nevertheless placed there to

13 - Parker, p26

learn domestic skills. Training was designed to develop 'self-reliance' and to equip inmates to become 'at least useful members of society'.[14] Gwen has described being at Warlies – whose motto was 'Cheer up and go on' – as 'the most dreadful experience any girl of that age could go through'. She writes: 'I was away from the Grimseys, my friends, and everything else that was familiar to me. We were taught how to do laundry, scrub floors, clean bedrooms, polish, and so on. It was hard physical work. There were about fifty girls sleeping in a number of dormitories. Many of them were distraught and cried every night. Some threatened to take their own lives, and some tried by jumping over the balcony at the top of the big winding staircase. A few girls ran away, but were soon returned accompanied by a policewoman'.[15] A tidy appearance was compulsory, girls were criticised for the smallest perceived transgression, and 'staff were cold and unfeeling'. Matron in particular was 'extremely cruel' and later dismissed after she was found to be an alcoholic drug-abuser.[16] For reasons that are unclear, blurred by the passing of years, Dolly arrived after a few weeks to take Gwen to London, where she was to live in the family home and start work in a watchmaker's workshop. 'I was more than happy to leave [Warlies]. Yet the idea of living with my birth mother, a woman I didn't know and hadn't seen for many years was, in itself, quite terrifying'.[17]

Gwen's unsympathetic view of Dolly is undoubtedly coloured by the lack of any warmth or affection in their subsequent relationship; she retains the perception that Dolly's actions were based on Gwen's ability to supplement the family's income rather than a desire to compensate for lost years, or to provide motherly love. Sadly, the question of Dolly's motivations will remain unanswered. Barnardo's acknowledges that many children in its care experienced loneliness, bullying and abuse, and that life under its auspices

....

14 – Warlies Park House website
15 – Pearce, *The Worst Weeks of My Life*, 2003
16 – Rose, p76
17 – Pearce, *The Worst Weeks of My Life*, 2003

A True Family

was, for some, an appalling experience leaving deeply felt wounds.[18] But although there were times of disruption and unhappiness in Gwen's childhood her abiding memories of the years spent with the Grimseys are extremely fond. She is ever grateful to Barnardo's – an organisation she continues to support – for providing her with a loving, secure family – in her view, a 'true family'. Leaving her birth mother behind led Gwen to a foster family which provided the love, care and emotional stability every child needs.

Gwen (far right) in 2010 with her husband and grandchildren

18 – Dr Barnardo's changed its name to Barnardo's in 1988 to reflect the break from its original Victorian values.

Bibliography

Barnardo's. Barnardo's Children. 2013. http://www.barnardos.org.
uk/barnardo_s_children_v2.pdf (accessed March 29, 2013).
The History of Barnardo's. 2013.

http://www.barnardos.org.uk/what_we_do/who_we_are/history.
htm (accessed March 28th, 2013).

The History of Barnardo's: 1845-1905 The work of Thomas Barnardo.
2013. www.barnardos.org.uk_s_history.pdf (accessed March 19,
2013).

Fletcher, Winston. *Keeping the Vision Alive: The Story of Barnardo's
1905-2005*. Ilford, Essex: Barnardo's, 2005.

Pearce, Gwen. *The Worst Weeks of My Life*. Barnardo's Guild
Messenger, 2003: 12.

Pearce, Gwen (2010, December 5th). Meeting at Gwen's home. (C.
Pearce, Interviewer).

Powell, Julie. Warlies Park House History. 2013. http://www.
warliesparkhouse.com/history.html (accessed April 4th, 2013).

R A Parker. *Away From Home: A Short History of Provision for
Separated Children*. Ilford, Essex: Barnardo's, 1990.

Rose, June. *For the Sake of the Children*. London: Hodder &
Stoughton, 1987.

All photos from Gwen Pearce's personal collection, reprinted with
permission.

....

Caroline Pearce is currently ghost-writing the autobiography of a Siberian camp survivor whose
homes have included a hut shared with goats in a Russian village and a luxurious Regent's
Park penthouse flat. Studying Biography and Creative Non-Fiction at UEA has complemented
Caroline's work in exploring slices of personal history in a wider context.

Jessica Reik

The Refrigerator and Green Room
Vignettes from a book-length memoir

The Refrigerator

The house smelled as it always had, of a crown roast in the top oven, a strudel in the bottom, and furniture redolent of four generations, social smoking, wet bathing suits settling into brocade chairs, the bergamot of my grandmother's 4711 embedded in the linen wallpaper. There were pieces of masking tape stuck to the moldings beside paintings and on the hardest surface of each chair and settee, side table and china. 'Jenny', it said on an unnecessarily long strip, adhered to a napkin covering a ransom of silver. 'Hester', it said on the glass face of the panoramic music box; others said 'SK' for Skinner, the auction house.

I took the newspaper out of its wrapper and brought it to the kitchen. 'Viola,' I yelled out, up the staircase, 'Are you there?' The house felt especially still, the faucet dripped at its usual rate; fruit-flies congregated above the box of compost.

I did the thing that came by reflex, which was to wander into the kitchen and simultaneously open the refrigerator and freezer doors. 'Go check the icebox,' my grandmother would say, no sooner than we had cleared the threshold into the red room, no matter how many months it had been since we had seen her last. That was her way of hugging us since she didn't like physical contact. 'See what's around. Plenty of steak and ice creeeam' – her articulation of dessert foods was always prolonged. My mother would roll her eyes and say something like, 'Mom, we just ate,' and Granny would say something like, 'So?' and by then my brother and I would already have taken off, racing over the French clay tile, through the dining room and the pantry, hoping Zuleika or Fatima or either of the Marys wasn't there so we didn't have to say hello and could just dig in to whatever it was we wanted.

The current refrigerator didn't have in it any of the things I always recall it full of – spheres of melon, roasted chickens from the Star, spirals of smoked salmon and the pumpernickel cocktail rounds that became edible only when layered with cream cheese. Instead, it contained only the non-perishables no one had bothered to throw out after my grandmother had died.

On the door were lists of phone numbers, in an unrecognizable variety of handwritings; mostly my aunt's and uncle's, I supposed, perhaps a nurse's. There were a few photographs of the family underneath business cards and eight magnets saying, *Eat it today, wear it tomorrow* in green and blue italics. Above all of these items, free of overlapping notes and numbers, was an embossed piece of paper that said 'DNR'. It was the Massachusetts Department of Health 'Do Not Resuscitate' Order, also palliatively called – in front of the backslash – 'Comfort Care.'

Nowhere on the form was any sort of detail about what exactly the 'COMFORT CARE/Do not Resuscitate Order Verification Protocol' was, only that it existed and that all assigned parties had agreed that the person named in boxes one, two and possibly, if they had a middle name, three, was to receive said protocol should the occasion occur, in the out-of-hospital-setting.

I checked the cupboards and found an unopened box of Pimm's orange-filled biscuits, and figured I might as well have a few, that the feel of my teeth breaking through the hard chocolate coating, sinking down into the cloud of starch before reaching the jam layer might make my grandmother – who always kept a box in her purse – seem less remote. I took my Pimm's and went into the room to read the newspaper before I sat down to write her eulogy.

Green Room

I looked through the doorway into the green room and out the French doors to the swimming pool beyond. Two ducks floated by. Neglected since the money had run out, the pool was now a thriving bog, complete with resident wildlife – Jesus Bugs, dead rodents, marsh marigolds in bloom beneath the diving board. In the periphery, on the bookshelf to the right of the doors I saw a swatch of yellow and walked towards it. *Edward Lear,* I thought, as the slant of the blue font came into view. And before I reached out to grab it, I could hear her say:

'Is this dying?' Granny said.

'No,' I said, 'I think this is living.'

'How can that be? It feels so terrible.'

'I know, Granny. I'm sorry. Can I get you another blanket?'

'Who *did* all of this to me?'

'No one did. It's just how life sometimes is. Do you want me to bring you anything?'

'No dear.'

Granny rubbed both of her knees and rocked back and forth on the hospital cot in the green room. Her movements were unlike any I had ever seen her make; they were girlish and spontaneous, without the awareness of anything outside of her own body. I wondered if she'd ever come back, or if this would be the *new* granny – this old sagging flesh with pigeon-toes and the mannerisms of a five year old.

A few minutes before, I had been walking behind my grandmother as we made our way – forty-six of my footsteps, a variable number of hers, lasting nine to ten minutes if she didn't stop to look out the window – into the kitchen for lunch. I had already prepared her food – unseasoned Dover sole and steamed spinach – which I anticipated her complaining about because it did not involve a piece of meat. While I was thinking about how to handle her inevitable request for mayonnaise – something that always gave her diarrhea – she collapsed onto the pantry counter, then on to me, then both of us down onto the floor. She vomited, her knees made grinding sounds that body parts shouldn't make, and for a moment, went absolutely silent and still. *'Fuck,'* I thought, *'She's having a stroke.'*

'Hello?' she said, shifting around on top of me.

'Hi, Granny. Let me help you up.' I could see that the left side of her body had gone slack.

'Just let me stay here. It's better.'

'It's not really better. I'm going to get you up.' I took a sateen tablecloth out of the dining room chest and a chair wide and sturdy enough to contain her girth and put the one on top of the other and somehow, with my nose buried in my shirt – the only place I found reprieve from all the smells that were comingling, now that she'd also shat herself – lifted Granny into the chair and dragged her across the tile to the green room.

'It smells good in here,' she said.

'Yes, it does. Shall we get you onto the bed?'

'I don't know. Do you think we can manage?'

'It will be easy, just watch.' It wasn't, in fact, at all easy, but by now I had learned that the only way to transfer my grandmother without dislocating a shoulder or pulling my lumbars was to brace her weight with my thigh and then sort of lower us both down at once, hoping that the slight toss at the end would turn out gentle.

Her rocking became more rapid and in addition to rubbing her knees my grandmother started moaning, as if from a deep place permeated by ineluctable distress.

'Granny, do you want some juice or something?'

'Hello?'

'Granny, it's me, Jessie. Are you OK?'

'What's happening to me? I think I'm dying.'

'I don't think you're dying but I think you've just had a stroke.'

'A stroke!'

'Yes.'

'Ghastly.'

The phone rang in the next room. I ignored it and went to get the Edward Lear book off the table – it had always been my grandmother's favorite.

It started up again, this time the maximum number of rings –

twenty-four in the state of Massachusetts – until the operator terminated the call. *Aunt Jenny,* I thought, *she's the only one who does that.*

'Hi, Jenny,' I said, the next time it rang, dragging the phone behind me across the floor. It was the 'long phone', as my grandmother called it – the one she'd bring out over the terrace and down to the edge of the pool in between the ladder step rails and make calls to her grandchildren or the butcher or whomever might be in the kitchen, to bring her that thing she was missing, midway through a lap.

'How did you know it was me?'

'Just a guess.'

'Lucielle called to say that she'd be late and you should go ahead and give Granny lunch.'

'OK,' I said. 'When will she be back?' At this point I knew I would have to tell my aunt what had happened. That my grandmother wasn't only *mine,* that she had children and people who might want things done and measures taken to keep her alive, against or not against her will, but in accordance with theirs.

'An hour or so.'

'I think Granny just had a stroke.'

'Doubtful. But I'll stop by anyhow. I just have to go to the bank.'

'OK,' I said.

I sat down on the edge of my grandmother's bed and fanned through the book looking for 'The Owl and the Pussy-Cat.'

'What was all that?' my grandmother asked.

'All what?'

'Who were you just talking to?'

'Jenny. She's coming over and we're going to take you to the hospital.'

'What? That's a bad idea.'

'I know, Granny. But we're not in charge. Jenny is going to call an ambulance.'

'An ambulance?'

'Yes, an ambulance.'

I rubbed her legs, making sure to avoid the areas that looked soiled. She reached down and grabbed for my hand and squeezed it as though doing so might somehow change the situation.

'Can't we just stay here and die?' she asked. 'It can be our secret, I promise not to tell Mother.' When my grandmother wanted to break a perceived rule, eat a second helping of dessert, or stay home from her old people's group, she called my aunt 'Mother'. 'Just this once?' she said.

While on the surface I might have been taking care of my demented grandmother in routine and physical ways, what I was really doing was helping to re-create a world she could recognize herself in. It was a world that had stopped existing fifty years ago, but to her was known and immediate. A world where she thought we were off to the Plaza for breakfast even though it was in New York and she lived in Boston; a world of junket and oyster crabs and Bonwit Teller, where her parents were alive and my grandmother was still married to my grandfather, and she was young and they were happy. This was a difficult delusion to maintain, but one I stopped knowing how not to do, because it's how my grandmother and I came to know each other. At moments when she was confronted with the reality that everyone else belonged to – a world of digitized noise and pre-packaged dinners and visits to doctors who said things like 'ninety-three' and 'Alzheimer's' and 'Coumadin' – my grandmother at first didn't recognize herself, and then when she did, when she knew she was no longer that young woman in a cotton lawn dress, she instantly wanted to die. And for this reason, I was not on board with the hospital or the ambulance or the inevitability of a catheter and I said, 'Sure Granny, just this once,' and started reading,

   'The Owl and the Pussy-Cat went to sea
   In a beautiful pea-green boat.'

. . . .

Jessica Reik is currently working on a familial memoir spanning four generations and multiple narrative threads – visits to Sigmund Freud, concealed Jewishness, mental illness, evenings at the opera – all converging in the dilapidated estate she lived in with her grandmother. Jessica writes mostly in vignette form, teaches yoga and goes fly-fishing with her father.

Dannielle Shaw

Summer, the Bonds, Nanny and Me

The following is an extract from a memoir that focuses on my grandmother and her relationship with her eccentric, titled, employer

Foreword

W hen I was born, my mother and I weren't very well: an infection, an illness, and a case of the mumps. Lady Bond, my grandmother's employer, decided to pay us a visit at Wexham Park Hospital, off the Uxbridge Road. She parked her personalised fern green Rover and walked up to the reception of maternity with the biggest bunch of peonies, where my nan heard her ask in her plummiest tone, 'Lady Jennifer Bond to see Miss Nicola Lambert.' Jennie was attired in full Minnie Mouse regalia, complete with velvet ears, a spotted red dress and a stick-on nose with whiskers that wiggled when she talked. She'd hired the outfit from The Party Shop that morning. Nan said she'd never been so embarrassed, but then thought back and decided that what Lady Bond had done, though Jennie didn't know it, had been very kind and generous: she moved the talking point, switched the focus, and made Nan, Mum and the nurses forget the elephant in the room.

*

Summer holidays meant mornings spent following Roger, the 80-year-old gardener who was missing his left thumb, around Lady Bond's orchard and rose garden. This would be followed by the self-invented game skippy steps, which entailed running and skipping behind Jazz, Lady Bond's sausage dog, across the bridge over the pond and back again. Afternoons were filled with topping up empty Robertson's Golden Shred jars with water and fallen rose petals, in the hope of making a wearable eau de toilette, or trying to catch a full grown koi with nothing but a goldfish net and a lily pad, or creating 'potions' from soil, fallen leaves and various debris found in rose beds and primrose bushes. Occasionally, Roger would pick a head from whichever plant he was tending to, put it behind my ear, and declare I was the 'bonniest wee gal' he'd ever seen, taking my hand and spinning me around so my dress would float outwards the way it did for Ginger Rogers. Other days I'd be on my own pottering around with a colouring book, an Etch-a-Sketch, or a yo-yo, until Nan called for me from the French patio doors, when elevenses or lunch was ready.

Sometimes, before lunch, I'd help Nan dust the books in Sir Kenneth's library, lingering over the titles that sounded most exotic: *Roxana, Antigone, Justine.* The scent of beeswax polish filled the room, whilst the overgrown foxgloves rapped at the window as they swayed in the breeze. Sir Kenneth collected Baccarat paperweights with millefiori designs, and Nan said I wasn't to touch them, because they were more expensive than I was. Instead, I was in charge of cleaning the aged, green banker's lamp that tilted its neck to peruse Sir Kenneth's letters nosily. But usually, I'd forget to dust and spend most of my time spinning the antique globe next to Sir Kenneth's desk – much to my grandmother's horror – or trying to use his official seal to sign my drawings of Jazz and Roger.

Lady Bond insisted I call her Auntie Jennie, or Jennie Toot Toot. She'd pick Nan and me up on my way to school, tooting twice outside the conifers on our front lawn. She'd drop me off, toot twice again, and drive Nan on to her house in Wayside Gardens in Gerrards Cross. Nan was Jennie's housekeeper. Auntie Jennie liked having me spend my summer holidays with her in her enormous bungalow and grounds. All her children had families of their own and her much older husband, Sir Kenneth, mainly stayed in his office. I'd rarely see Sir Kenneth, not even for lunch. He'd occasionally make an appearance when he needed Nan to run an errand, or when she happened to be baking meringues. Though Sir Kenneth rarely spoke to me, he insisted on buying me a new dress every Christmas. He'd buy London's finest: labels that Nan and I didn't know and would never be able to pronounce, or afford.

Come June, Nan and I would stay at Jennie's house when she went on her annual holiday to Ibiza. Whilst she was away, Jennie insisted we made ourselves at home. We would share bubble baths in her enormous circular spa tub, and Nan would relax in Sir Kenneth's electronic recliner, giggling as she'd play with the buttons, feigning shock and surprise when it moved back and forth, or began its 'pulsating massage' on setting number four. Meanwhile, I watched *The Herbs* and *Watch with Mother*. I especially liked *Picture Book*, because Sausage reminded me of Jazz, Jennie's dog, and I could pretend I was the pretty woman with the puppet teaching children different activities: lantern-making or growing mustard and cress. This formed the basis of my school holidays for the best part of five years, until Jennie accidentally ran Jazz over. Jennie refused to wear her glasses for driving, and didn't see Jazz coming as she backed out of the garage. Nanny explained that some women didn't like to wear their glasses because they thought it spoiled their face. I thought it was ridiculous to think that something as silly as glasses could make you unattractive, and that I'd rather be unattractive wearing glasses with a sausage dog, than be pretty, without glasses, and sausage dog-less. That Christmas I got a posh dress and Jennie got a poodle.

Jennie Bond's garden was so big that Nan always had a fresh and varied supply of flowers to use in furnishing the house and creating a centrepiece for the dining table. In Sir Kenneth's office, she'd choose small flowers that didn't drop their pollen. Vases of roses or crocuses were pushed to the corner of a grey filing cabinet, or centred on the deep windowsill and exchanged every few days. Jennie always had a posy of daffodils in March (Nan's favourite) and tulips in April: always the two-tone hybrids she'd had imported from Holland. My favourite chore was helping Nan to arrange the flowers for the drawing room. Here were the tallest, most exotic displays: gladioli, irises, hollyhocks, peonies, Black Knight and Guinevere delphiniums, echinacea, gypsophila and verbena. The room was peppered with smaller vases of chrysanthemums, lilies, and freesias, all filling the room with their delicate scents. I liked gerberas best; they were bright and slender without being too showy, and if the water needed changing, or needed a little sugar, the gerberas lowered their heads forlornly, as if to tell you.

Jennie collected Capodimonte, porcelain antiques. I wasn't to go near them. On the rectangular glass coffee table, on top of a lace doily, a large Capodimonte special edition, *The Cheats*, was centred. It depicted a group of boys playing cards at a round table, as one of the boys secretly passes a ten of diamonds under the table to the boy opposite with his toes. A young girl looks on and the boy receiving the card has his forefinger pushed against his lips. I was allowed to touch this one, but only because my fingers were small enough to get into the creases and clean the specks of dust from the edge of the cards. If Jennie and Sir Kenneth were out, Nan would listen to the radio, or put her favourite record on the oak-encased player in the drawing room. She loved Maria Callas and Nat King Cole. We'd be vinegar-washing French windows, or elbow-deep in soapy water scrubbing the grouting between black and white diamond tiles, listening to Maria Callas in Bellini's *Norma* and I'd be thinking of afternoon picnics and evening strolls with Nan and Grandad, and Nan would be thinking the same, though she'd pause and state unrelated details like, 'Sausages tonight,' and, 'I think we'll be done before three.' When she paused, she'd put her hand to her head and wipe away a cotton-white curl from her brow, as her gold-plated Rotary watch twisted round her wrist so the face turned inwards. She didn't clock-watch, but I suppose this helped.

On the last Saturday in summer holidays Nan would pack a picnic and take me on the train from Gerrards Cross to London. Mood-dependent, we would venture to the Natural History Museum, the

V and A, or visit the zoo at Regent's Park, often stopping for a walk in Green Park, near to Helena Rubinstein's, where Nan worked as a secretary when she was a girl. Nan was the one who'd send out free samples of the perfumes. Green Velvet was her favourite, but they stopped selling it in the 1970s, and Nan resorted to wearing Lily of the Valley instead. If we had time, when we were in the area, we'd stop in Chelsea, where Nan's Aunt Alice used to live. She had owned a Victorian terraced house and Nan said that when Alice died, they converted it into flats. Alice had lived on Slaidburn Street, near the World's End pub off the King's Road. Charles Booth had once declared it 'one of the worst streets in Chelsea and I should say one of the worst in London – drunken, rowdy, constant trouble to police: many broken patched windows, open doors, drink-sodden women at windows.' But Nan said I'd be doing all right if I got an SW postcode. Her other aunt, Mabel, had lived round the corner on Blantyre Street. We'd visit the houses, and then the Chelsea Cinema, and she'd tell me how it used to be called the Gaumont Theatre, back in the 1940s. Nan didn't seem to mind that all of the mothers with children were half her age; she could get concession prices.

If that Saturday were sunny, we'd always go to Kew. We'd sit at the same place every trip, near the rhododendrons by the Pagoda, and Nan would hand me a bottle of cloudy lemonade, or ginger beer, and we'd share cheese and pickle sandwiches, with day-old fairy cake for afters. Nan would punctuate the swallowing of mouthfuls by naming numerous species of birds and plants, making sure to tell me which were Grandad's favourites. He worked weekdays and weekends at the dairy, so he was never able to join us on our London excursions. Nan liked the Canadian Geese, but I wasn't so fond because they kept pinching my sandwiches when Nan's back was turned. Nan gave the geese her sandwiches freely, and said Grandad liked nothing better than feeding the birds. I knew then that I wanted my husband to be able to tell the difference between martins and warblers, monkshood and bluebells. Nanny said you could tell a lot about a man by his interest in wildlife: if he was good-natured he'd like swifts (my favourites), if he were ill-tempered he'd not indulge your question.

Nanny said I was to make sure that *my* husband liked swifts, because by the time I got married, she might not be around to check.

. . . .

Dannielle Shaw was born in Buckinghamshire, where her grandparents raised her. She studied English Literature at UEA before completing the MA in Biography and Creative Non-Fiction. Dannielle's interests lie with historical fiction and biography, with a particular interest in eighteenth-century London.

Naomi Spicer

The Lie Behind the Beauty of Death

Have you ever seen someone die? Because I can tell you it's nothing like the movies. It's not romantic, or meaningful, or beautiful. At least my experience wasn't. And whenever I'm watching films, I can't help but feel cheated at what they made my expectations of death to be. They gave me a false sense of security. Because it's nothing like that. The image of seeing my father die in front of me will never, ever leave my mind.

Don't get me wrong, I never thought it would be a memory that I would easily wipe, but that image is so concrete, so sharp, so clear in my head. And the films didn't prepare me for that. I wanted to shout that dead people look nothing like their stupid films. I wanted to scream that they don't look peaceful, they don't look rosy and their cheeks don't remain full of colour or their cheekbones tinted.

The reality? The colour drains from their face as the blood stops circulating their veins. The blood stands still and just lies in the tubes, still like a milk pond. No movement. No oxygen. No pumping.

And then the spirit takes the heat from the body, leaving just the nape of the neck slightly warm. And you watch your mother holding the nape and screaming to keep the doors and windows shut; keep the heat in, keep him in, just for as long as you can.

Don't let him get cold. Because that would be reality.

That would be reality smashing in, and you coming to the realisation that he has left.

What did death look like? It looked grey and cold with a green tint. It looked sparse and bare. But most of all? It looked like a monster had stolen my father's body. It looked like something had eaten its way through his frame and ripped the most worthy man from underneath us. And what was left when his spirit departed the skeleton? Just the organs transformed by this disgusting, vile, unforgiving thing that stole my father.

*

It was a sunny bank holiday and Dad had proposed that we went sailing for the day. Nothing out of the ordinary. Sailing was a part of my childhood and I relished the chance to spend a day reliving it. So we set off: my mum, dad, younger brother and sister and I.

In opposing boats we danced on the waves, we ducked and dived, we raced, we laughed, and we fell in. With the occasional warning and instruction being yelled from Dad, I was untouchable. I was on the water with my father; I was home. The wind blessed us and stayed constant, giving us the occasional change of direction to play with and my mother stood on the banks worriedly shouting exclamations when she felt my father was pushing it too close. But my dad knew what he was doing.

As the cool evening air started to set in, we stored the boats and headed towards the car. We shuffled awkwardly behind the car doors, trying to change out of our wet clothes whilst preserving our dignity. As far as I was concerned, if you managed to get your feet out of the wet-shoes that had suctioned to your feet, and then dry them and put on fresh socks and shoes without falling over or getting the gravel in between your toes then it was a miracle. I looked up and saw us all struggling, with towels and clothes sporadically appearing and falling. It was a sight to behold. And in that moment I felt so high; that feeling that buzzes around your heart and you can't help feeling overwhelmed with happiness; like everything was in the right place. I slept so soundly that night.

The next day we were eating lunch outside. My dad took the plates into the kitchen.

'I'll do it Dad!'

'No Naomi, I'd like to do it.' I laughed about how silly he was being. The look on Mum's face was funny. She looked awkward but there was sadness behind her eyes. It was one of those looks that you don't properly engage with until you can see with hindsight. Her heart must have been wrenching out of her chest as I joked so innocently, unaware of what was about to happen.

When Dad returned, he sighed, looked at Mum, looked back and then spoke. Before any words had even come out of his mouth I couldn't breathe.

And that was it. My dad had cancer. The one-in-three had happened to us. My family was now a statistic. Just like that my whole world broke apart. I now realised why yesterday had been so perfect. He'd manufactured the perfect memory; a day which epitomised our relationship and childhood; which made us realise how much he loved us. I felt almost angry that he'd created such a perfect moment to ruin; but overwhelmed at his thought process.

Those two days defined my father completely. He had an innate ability to succeed at anything he put his mind to, he was a brilliant teacher who always knew exactly what to say and stayed calm and collected. He would never unnecessarily worry or hurt us, and he was thoughtful beyond belief. He was a fighter. And I guess that it was for those reasons that I sunk into the belief that he would fight this too. I was a victim of ignorance. I thought he would win.

It was three days before Christmas 2011 that we got the test results following the six months of chemo. It hadn't worked. There was nothing they could do. The prognosis had been deemed terminal.

Something changed after that, obviously so, but it was more about the way that we saw things. I still believed that he would live for at least a year, but then he started getting really poorly. Previously when he was ill we saw it as the chemo working, the chemo making him ill. Now when he was ill we saw the cancer eating away inside him. I imagined it as a monster eating him from the inside out, and nightmares succeeded these imaginations. We were about to watch him die.

The most frustrating thing is expectation. As you grow up you talk about bucket lists. With friends you discuss what you might do if you were given an average of a year to live. Would you travel the world, do crazy things, drive down Route 66? But the reality is Dad had to go to hospital once a week for chemo injections, blood tests or scans. He had a nurse on call at all times, and he could never be more than half an hour's drive from the hospital. He couldn't have done anything on a bucket list even if he'd had one. Because the cancer, in reality, had already won.

In July I graduated; and he attended, albeit wheelchair-bound and having to leave as soon as the ceremony finished. He set about getting ready to die. He even started designing his coffin.

He knew; he accepted the deal and I didn't. In August he travelled to Venice with my mum and brother. Mum had lists of all of the local hospitals on her at all times. Dad seemed well, he could walk. They watched a string quartet playing *Titanic* under the stars in a quaint Italian courtyard and Dad stood behind my mum as she flung her arms out and shouted,

'Look Jack, I'm flying!' My mum ushered my six-foot tall brother to be the mast of the boat, but he politely refused and tried to hide anywhere he possibly could out of sight; a mean feat when you look like the Big Friendly Giant. Dad joked with Mum, he walked for miles around Venice, he ate out and he slept well and he lived.

Two days after they returned he was rushed into hospital for an operation because his bowel had kinked. He was given a colostomy bag and put on even more drugs. He was also told that if it happened again they wouldn't be able to operate. This was it.

I was in Norwich when Mum rang from the hospice. I asked her to put Facetime on so that I could see Dad for myself and decide how well he looked. *That* is one of the images. His eyes rolled back into his head sporadically, he couldn't make sense of what was being said, and his lip dropped to one side like he'd had a stroke. I had to go home. I'd seen him forty-eight hours earlier and he'd been talking and active. Within three days the doctors' estimate had turned from months, to weeks, to days, to hours. A day later I texted my dad's best friend:

'Wilber, it's not looking good. They reckon hours left.' He came the next morning, with his son, one of my closest and oldest friends, and he sat in that room with Dad for twelve hours. By this point my dad couldn't talk. Wilber's son, Alex, sat on the sofa and stroked my hair as I lay in his lap. I fell asleep within seconds. I hadn't slept for days and the comfort of having Alex with me took over.

My father died on Tuesday evening. I'd sat with him until four o'clock Tuesday morning through him intermittently waking from his drug-induced slumber shouting through a coarse throat, 'help me', and writhing in pain. I called for the nurse every time and occasionally they administered more painkillers. They had increased his level of painkillers to a point where, in theory, he wouldn't feel the pain but his level of consciousness would also be reduced. I don't know if he knew I was there. Tuesday daytime he briefly woke and slurred,

'Where's Naomi?' I was heartbroken. He thought I wasn't there for him. Mum assures me that it was just because he was confused. His brain was fumbling to stay living and his mind was struggling to stay clear but it was fighting against strong drugs and disease. To this day, I still wonder whether he knew I was there. And when I think about it, the panic sets deep in my stomach that he might have died thinking I wasn't there for him.

'We're all here Daddybear. We're all right here. Naomi, Amelia, Alex, and me.'

'I ... love ... you.'

'We love you too.'

*

It happened when I was drinking a chocolate cream frappuccino from Starbucks brought by my friend. My auntie walked into the common room and simply said, 'You need to come. Now.' And that was it. I walked in to that picture that was so different from what the movies showed. You could see he had gone. His body was just an empty corpse.

I'm not sure if I believe in God. I don't believe in ghosts, and I've always been unsure about spirits, but as I sat in the chair next to that body I felt a hand on my shoulder, I felt his warmth. I could physically see him. Something distracted me, and then he was in the garden. He was getting further away. He was standing under the massive oak tree in the garden outside his room. The boughs of the tree loomed over him and the lush grass gave him a soft standing place. I could see the whole garden, and I knew he wasn't there, and yet I could see him.

For the next two weeks, before the funeral, I saw him and felt him with me.

When my Dad asked me where I wanted him to die I said not at home. I dreaded that image. It turns out I was wrong. Where he died wasn't his choice in the end, but the image of his body surrounded by wires and machines and unknown items was worse. That scene, that moment, those fifty-six hours will never leave me. Every time I walk into his bedroom I see him sitting there. It doesn't matter where it happened because the image is the same; just a different backdrop. And I guess that's the thing about death; it never leaves you.

. . . .

Naomi Spicer was born and raised in Shakespeare's Warwickshire. After studying her BA she went straight on to her MA, and now plans to travel, whilst writing freelance. Naomi's interests lie outside the constraints of straight biography, so far having written pieces about the sex lives of students, the life of abused horses and mini snap-shot biographies.

Alexis Wolf

The Mother Lode

'The smell of the blackberry is sweeter than any perfume you can buy,' my father repeated, 'and it should certainly be bottled.' I smile at him in agreement, though we both understand it will remain forever impossible to duplicate the way the ripe fruit smells in Washington State at the height of August.

The branches of the bush, the white flowers with prickly extensions, the hot days when the blackberries are so heavy that they drip off the vine and into the seat of your palm. It is sweet yet thorny, a system of learning how and when to pluck, how to carry yourself through a danger that will bring an obvious reward. The red juice coats the scratches left by the brambles like a thick layer of sweet summer blood. In my family the blackberry is more than a summertime treat, it is a ritual that has taken on all the weight of any other holiday from the yearly festival calendar.

For my father, this takes the form of the often surprising realization that his body is more entwined with the earth than suburban living might daily suggest. The protection of the wilderness still exists in our tame climate in the shape of this prize.

Today is my father's birthday, and the sun is streaming down on the backs of our necks in the empty bank parking lot. The saucepans and mixing bowls that we brought from home are beginning to fill up with the soft ripe fruits, but my father keeps reaching his tools past the easy spots and deep into the back of the bush. With a pair of gardening clippers and a short-handled rake, he snaps off the branches of the invasive species and brings back a vine covered in a ready yield. We are collecting the essential ingredients for the annual birthday pie.

A woman walking by on the sidewalk with her daughter stares at us across the pavement of the parking lot. The look on her face is a cross between intrigue and condemnation.

'Come and join us!' My father bellows. But the woman decides against it, tightens her grip on her small daughter's wrist and pulls her off around the corner. We must look like common thieves here, but really we are just collecting what is rightly ours.

My father is unfazed by this passing stranger's disapproval. 'We've hit the mother lode,' he declares with a childlike delight. My father's lips open to accept a perfect berry inside, the holy summer offering exploding on his tongue. He uses the tools to position the branches for me so that I can stand almost inside the bush and reach the ripest bits. He makes it safe by snipping away the dead parts of the plant; soon I'm nearly enclosed by the sharp prickly protrusions that exact the cost of such a free bounty. He holds back the tendrils so that I can insert a small and sneaky hand further inside and carefully harvest our dearest of treasures. It's as if I am a child again, only now that I am a full grown woman, I am a more agile partner, and indeed we form a better and stronger team. For I have learned the prescribed sanctions of this practice well, though my father still chooses to repeat them frequently to me as we gather, as if I haven't been trained specifically for this activity. He controls every movement that I make inside the bush, but for once, I do not mind his brand of micromanagement, and I feel safe. I understand that this is where he does business. When I join him here, my need to assert my identity as a person rather than a daughter evaporates into the edges of our shared familial altar.

The bishop of the berry bush, at home in his responsibilities, we review but not revise: 'You never step upon a berry,' he instructs me. 'You never pull the berry from the branch, it must be ready enough to fall into your hand upon touching it. And most importantly, you leave the lowest fruit for little children, who might come after you.'

When I was young the blackberry bushes snagged my soft white skin and I would cry. My father encouraged patience, and demonstrated by example his reverie for the vines. He spoke to them in the same deep voice he reserved for the enormous trees that he would meet on rare visits to the forest of our northwestern territory. He was a stranger there but he would saunter up along the giants and rap their sides with his open palm and say in his loudest and manliest voice, 'look at this big guy!' His face delighting in an unusual and enraptured smile. The blackberry bushes that he still tames enlist the same deep and booming voice, the same devout and awed posture. Sighing into the thorns he basks in nature as if we come from a family of farmers. No one would expect this of my father who, though possessing his own oddities, appears to be a fairly normal and even-keeled man upon first meeting. He rarely breaks the rules and so every August I delight to see him gathering the gifts from nature that particularly delight him. He is transformed into a sage as he completes this act that verges on vagrancy, but that he considers an inheritance.

We have never been a tribe of gardeners, at least for as long as my father can remember. Our fingers are not familiar with the soil. For my father, the act of picking berries holds a consecrated meaning that exists outside of any capitalist structure. His long-time existence as a labored worker who fought hard to find his place in the middle of America does not cloud his pleasure. The ripe goods are special, because they are owned by no one and by everyone, the red juice coating our fingers is a contract and a promise that some of the most valuable assets are free from monetary obligation. Typically, we would never be displaced into the realm of hunters or gatherers, our suburban foothold so entrenched that this act of natural transgression became all the more full of power.

Fresh off the boat from a far away world, my grandparents hadn't looked for bushes or fields, but rather accepted bits of charity until they could buy into the dream of a subdivision. Not city dwellers, and not country folk. It was a middle ground agreed upon by the incongruity of their union and reconciled by a compromise of origins. My grandfather had come from rural poverty, and my grandmother from a bustling urban center. Together they began anew in America and their daily acts of want gave way to a pact of muted prosperity.

Their displacement training skills began to put the meat onto the table, and inserted them into the strangeness of the suburbs. Nothing grew unrestrained in their new and carefully molded neighborhood, save for the blackberry bushes thronging in the empty lot across the street. It was the only plot of land left without a tidy new house, as if the developers had felt an obligation to leave a patch of wilderness for the children who were to come of age in this cookie cutter environment. In that lot my father paid the price for the freedom afforded to his boyhood in blood, stepping on beehives full of angry inhabitants and falling head first into unrelenting brambles. But the rewards were always sweeter than the penance.

As my grandparents struggled to achieve and make their lives not only comfortable but abundant as the first generation in a new country, every penny counted. But the lot across the street offered a respite from the strains of capitalism that bit down into their efforts; free berries every summer, like a giving tree for the American dream. Despite the fact that the task of picking reduced the family from skilled blue collar workers into agricultural laborers who sweat in the sun, the act was somehow mystical. Their son, my father, came bounding into the kitchen with a saucepan full of berries. For once, nothing was borrowed, nothing was bought, earned or sold. Just a karmic offering to ease any lingering anxieties with a sweetness offered up by the season. And the berries helped heal the halted words in the struggling house by becoming a part of the yearly routine. Despite starting a foreign pattern of home in a brand new land, traditions were formed that felt as old as the earth. And now in the month of August, it is forever known that together as a family we dine upon creation.

An invasive species gave us our license for bonding. We made a treaty with the thorns through their rare dreamlike flavor. In my mind it is as a blessed inclosure, because it is the nebulous place where we make peace.

Still standing in the sun, he wields the rake and clippers. He controls the motions. His blood flows calm and we are full of love for something. Maybe for each other. Maybe for the season. We've long forgotten the fights of my youth, and we are focused drunkenly on the generous tide of this voluptuous moment. We pluck the last few blackberries because our bowls are spilling over, and climb back into the car to go and make the birthday pie. The excitement of the summer and the delight at having performed our annual act of worship are coursing through our veins. My father can hardly believe the luck of the harvest, and as he turns the key in the ignition, his face is all alight with pure satisfaction. 'It was the mother lode,' he repeats, 'today we hit the mother lode.'

. . . .

Alexis Wolf is originally from Seattle. Her published work includes non-fiction reflective of Jewish-American family life and articles focused on extraordinary women in the nineteenth century. Her current project, a full-length biography of Anglo-Irish sisters Katherine and Martha Wilmot, explores the lives of female travellers in the Romantic era.